P9-DGB-446
A11905 845110

The Library of SPIDERS™

The Black Widow

Alice B. McGinty

The Rosen Publishing Group's
PowerKids Press™
New York

For Zachary

Published in 2002 by The Rosen Publishing Group, Inc.
29 East 21st Street, New York, NY 10010

First Edition

Book Design: Emily Muschinske
Project Editor: Emily Raabe
Project Consultant: Kathleen Reid Zeiders

Photo Credits: cover, title page © George Lepp/CORBIS; p. 5 (silhouettes), p. 18 (above) © Alan Morgan/Peter Arnold; p. 5 (inset) © James H. Robinson/Animals Animals; pp.6 (upper left), 13 (lower right), 14 (lower left) © Animals Animals; p.6 (center) © Fabio Colombini/Animals Animals; pp. 6,10 (microscopic photos) © Jim Zuckerman/CORBIS; pp. 9 (left), 10 (right) © Bill Beatty/Animals Animals; p. 9 (right) © Roger Rageot/David Liebman; p. 13 (left) © Jack Clark/Animals Animals; p. 13 (upper right),17 (center), 21 © David Liebman; p.14 (upper left) © James Gerholdt/Peter Arnold; p. 14 (upper right) © D. Thompson/Animals Animals; p. 17 (bottom left) © Norbert Wu/Peter Arnold; p. 17 upper right © Doug Wechsler/Animals Animals; p. 18 (bottom left) © Robert Noonan.

McGinty, Alice B.
The black widow spider / Alice B. McGinty.—1st ed.
p. cm.— (The library of spiders)
ISBN 0-8239-5565-6 (lib. bdg.)
1. Black widow spider—Juvenile literature. [1. Black widow spider. 2. Spiders.] I. Title.
QL458.42.T54 M44 2002
595.4'4—dc21 00-011690

Manufactured in the United States of America.

Contents

The Black Widow

The female black **widow** is the most **poisonous** spider in North America. Why is she called a black widow? It was believed that the female black widow always ate her mate, leaving herself a widow. In truth female black widows don't usually eat their mates. Once in a while they may mistake their mates for **prey** and eat them.

The adult female black widow measures about one and a half inches (4 cm) long. She is shiny and black with a dark red **hourglass** shape on her **abdomen**. The male black widow is much smaller than the female.

Did You Know?

The male black widow doesn't have an hourglass shape on his abdomen. He is also not poisonous, and is not known to bite people.

(Left) The female black widow has an hourglass shape on her abdomen. The male is small and pale with different markings.

(Top right) This photograph shows a female black widow (above) and the much smaller male widow (below).

spinnerettes

striped markings

(Top) This shows a black widow making a web. The spinnerettes release silk for the web.

(Right) This is what a spider looks like under a microscope. The green bumps are the spider's eyes. You can see the hair on the spider's legs in this photograph.

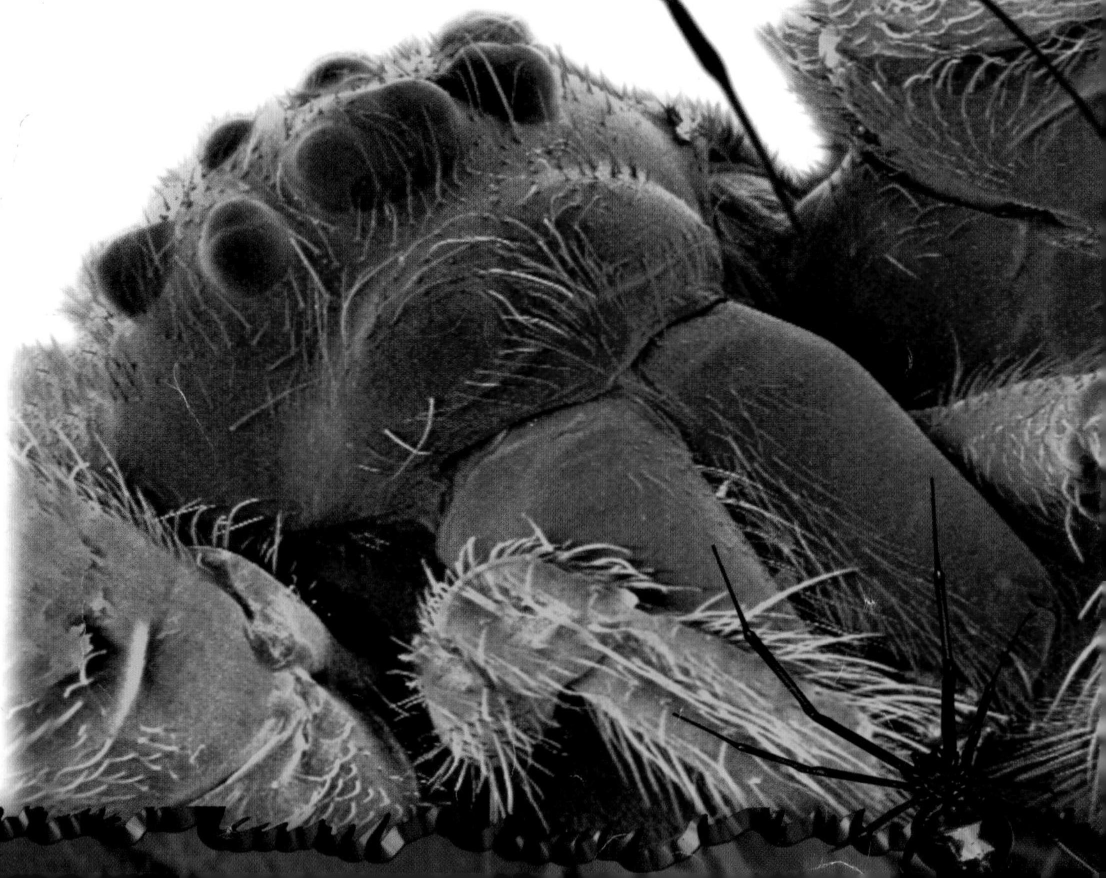

Cobweb Weavers

Scientists divide plants and animals into smaller groups so they can study them. Black widows belong to the **family** of comb-footed spiders, or cobweb weavers. The comb-footed spider's web is a messy maze of silk threads known as a cobweb. Comb-footed spiders all have comblike hairs on their legs. These hairs help the spiders build webs and wrap their prey in silk.

Black widows also belong to a smaller group. This group, the **genus**, is called ***Latrodectus***. Other widow spiders, like brown and bed widows, are part of this genus, too. The genus is divided into even smaller groups called **species**. Spiders in the same species are very much alike. There are five species of black widows in North America. Many of them live in the southern part of the United States.

The Black Widow's Body

Black widows have two main body parts. The rear body part is the abdomen. The heart, lungs, silk **glands**, and digestive organs are in the abdomen. The front body part is called the **cephalothorax**. It contains the poison **glands**, brain, and stomach.

All spiders have eight legs. Black widows have three claws on each leg to help them grasp strands of silk. Two **feelers**, called **pedipalps**, help black widows hold their prey. Two jaws end in sharp fangs. Spiders use these fangs to inject a poison, also called venom, into their prey.

Did You Know?

Spiders are covered in a hard shell called an exoskeleton. This shell protects the spider like a suit of armor.

(Left) This black widow is holding the silk for its web with one leg.

(Below) This black widow has unusual coloring. Its cephalothorax is red instead of black.

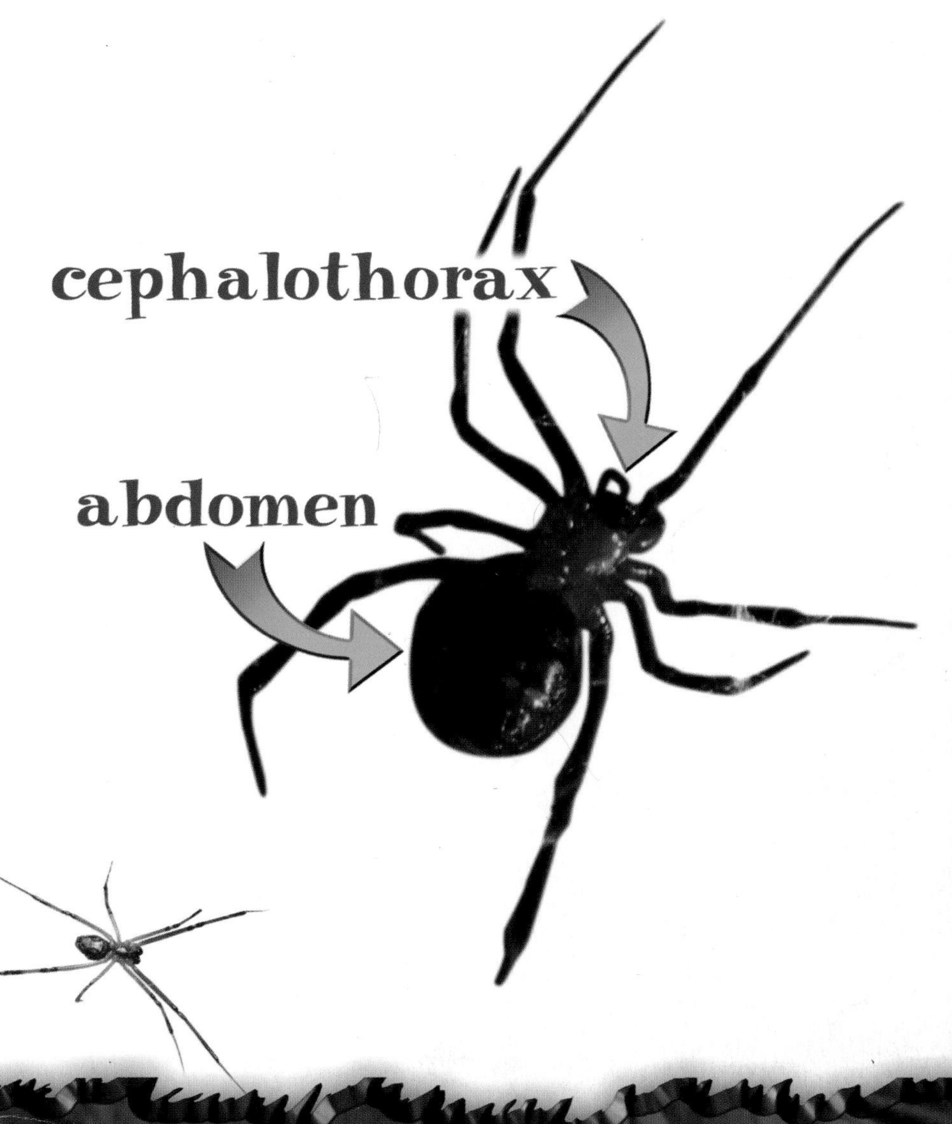

(Top left) This shows the pedipalp of the black widow.

(Top right) This shows the spider's abdomen. The hole beneath the hourglass marking is where the silk comes out.

(Left) This image shows what a black widow's eyes look like up close.

How the Black Widow's Body Works

Although black widows have eight eyes, they cannot see well. They cannot see colors or any shapes. Black widows only use their eyes to detect motion. Tiny hairs on their legs sense vibrations, sounds, and movements in the air. These hairs are very sensitive. They can even sense the beating of a fly's wings. Spiders taste food with special hairs on their feet and their feelers. When the spider dips these hairs into liquid, the spider can taste the liquid.

Spiders need oxygen to live, but they don't breathe like people. Spiders have slits, or openings, in their abdomens. Air seeps in and out through these slits.

A Spider's Web

Did You Know?

The black widow makes repairs to her web almost every day. She eats the damaged silk and replaces it with new silk.

Black widows build their webs in dark, quiet places, such as under stones or logs, or in and around old buildings.

To begin their web, black widows release silk from their **spinnerettes**. They attach the silk to a surface and lower themselves to another surface. By stretching its silk between the two surfaces, the spider builds its web. Black widows' silk comes out as liquid. The spider combs the silk with its legs into a sturdy thread. In about an hour, its web is finished. There is a thick silk pocket in one area of the cobweb. This is the spider's hideout.

spinnerettes

Black widows use different types of silk for building webs, wrapping insects, and making egg sacs. Their silk can be fuzzy or smooth, thick or thin, dry, or sticky.

(Top right) This is a picture of the tangled cobweb that black widows make.

(Left, top and bottom) These black widows are wrapping up their meals of a grasshopper and a yellow ant.

Trapping Food

A vibration in its web tells the black widow that it has caught an insect. The spider quickly backs up to the insect, throws silk on it, and wraps it up so that it cannot move. The spider bites the insect with its fangs. Then it injects the insect with venom to kill it.

Special juices in the spider's venom turn the insides of the insect to liquid. The black widow sucks out the liquid. Several hours later, the only thing left of the insect is an empty shell.

Black widows eat almost anything that gets trapped in their webs. Some of their most common foods are beetles, flies, June bugs, grasshoppers, moths, or even other spiders.

Laying Eggs

A male taps a female's web. He shakes his abdomen to vibrate the web. This signals to the female that he wants to **mate**. If the female is ready to mate, she will return the signal to the male. After mating, the male leaves quickly. Otherwise the female might mistake him for a meal.

The female's abdomen swells with growing eggs. She spins three or four sturdy bowls of silk. Then she lays her eggs in the bowls. She covers the eggs with sticky silk and turns the bowls over until they are round sacs. She attaches the egg sacs to her web and guards them.

Did You Know?

Each one of the black widow's egg sacs contains between 240 and 750 tiny white eggs. Only 1 to 12 young spiders will survive from each egg sac.

swollen
abdomen

(Top) These photos show female black widows and their egg sacs.

(Bottom left) This female black widow is swollen with eggs.

(Top) A black widow guards her egg sacs.

(Left) Tiny spiderlings do not have any hair or claws when they are born. After they molt, their new skin will be colored like an adult spider.

Baby Spiders

The black widow's eggs hatch several weeks after being laid. Baby spiders are called spiderlings. Inside the egg sacs, the spiderlings molt, or shed their skin. When they are ready, the pale spiderlings tear a hole in the cocoon. They step out one by one. They are in danger. They may be eaten by birds or insects, by their mother, or even by each other.

The spiderlings climb up high on the web. They release silk from their spinnerettes. Breezes catch the silk and carry the spiderlings away. This is called ballooning. The spiderlings build their webs wherever they land. As the spiderlings grow, they molt again. Their hard **exoskeleton** splits and they step out. Their bodies grow until their new skin hardens.

The Black Widow's Enemies

Many birds, frogs, insects, and even other spiders eat black widows. Mud dauber wasps sting black widows so that the spider cannot move. Then the wasp lays an egg on the helpless spider and buries it alive. When the egg hatches, the baby wasp eats the spider.

If nothings eats them first, female black widows can live up to a year and a half. They usually die after their spiderlings hatch. Most male black widows live less than six months. Their search for a mate uses up all their time and energy.

Did You Know?

Black widows can die when it is very cold. They must find a warm, safe spot to survive the winter.

(Top) The mud dauber wasp is one of the black widow's enemies.

(Right and below) This photograph shows praying mantises about to eat their black widow dinners.

Black Widows and People

Black widows are shy around people. Female black widows only bite if they feel threatened and have no place to hide. Male black widows are not known to bite people.

The bite of a female black widow causes muscles to tighten, especially in a person's chest and abdomen. Most people recover in a few days, though a few people have died from black widows' venom. Fortunately there are treatments for black widow bites. Anyone who is bitten should see a doctor immediately.

Black widows are sometimes a bother to people when they build their webs close to, or in people's homes. By eating insects,though, black widows help keep the insect population low. In this way, these shy spiders are very helpful to people.

Glossary

abdomen (AB-duh-min) A spider's larger, rear body part.
cephalothorax (sef-uh-low-THOR-axks) A spider's smaller, front body part, containing its head.
exoskeleton (ek-oh-SKEH-lah-ton) The hard outer shell of a spider's body.
family (FAM-lee) The scientific name of a large group of plants or animals that are alike in some ways.
genus (JEE-nes) The scientific name of a group of similar plants or animals. Members of the same genus are always also members of the same family.
glands (GLANDS) A part inside the body that takes certain substances from the blood and changes them into chemicals that the body uses or gives off.
hourglass (OWER-glas) A timekeeper that has two parts connected by a narrow neck, where sand takes one hour to fall from the upper to the lower part.
Latrodectus (lah-troh-DEK-tus) The name, meaning biting robber, of a genus of spiders.
mate (MAYT) When a pair of animals join together to make babies.
pedipalps (pe-deh-PALPZ) Two short feelers attached to the cephalothorax.
poisonous (POY-zun-us) Something that can make you very sick or kill you.
prey (PRAY) An animal that is hunted by another animal for food.
species (SPEE-sheez) A group of living things that have certain basic things in common.
spinnerettes (spin-uhr-ETZ) Organs located on the rear of the spider's abdomen which release silk.
widow (WIH-doh) A woman whose husband has died.

Index

Web Sites

To learn more about black widows, check out these Web sites:

www.sfzoo.org/map.insectzoo.html
www.desertusa.com/july97/du_bwindow.html